Classics for the Advancing Pianist

Edward MacDowell

Edited by

NANCY BACHUS

Late Intermediate

to Early Advanced

Repertoire

Alfred Music
P.O. Box 10003
Van Nuys, CA 91410-0003
alfred.com

ISBN-10: 1-4706-2699-3
ISBN-13: 978-1-4706-2699-0

Cover art: The Catskills (1859) by Asher Brown Durand (American, 1796–1886), oil on canvas

Edward and Marian MacDowell (1886)

Contents

Preface

The *Classics for the Advancing Pianist* series provides motivating, enjoyable literature of substantial quality for developing keyboard artists, ordered in a logical progression from volume to volume. Edward MacDowell, an important composer of the late Romantic period, is represented in this book. His music spans a variety of moods and technical challenges, making these collections exciting to explore. The selections in these volumes are standard teaching repertoire and will help build technique and musicianship, as well as offer hours of personal enjoyment.

Edward MacDowell

Edward MacDowell (1860–1908) is one of the few composers whose fame was greater during his lifetime than it is today. Acclaimed as both a composer and pianist, he was one of the first Americans to gain international recognition for his music. At the turn of the 20th century, MacDowell was considered to be America's leading "modern" composer, but today his music is regarded as an extension of the 19th-century Romantic style. As a result, his piano music has been relatively neglected.

Many of MacDowell's piano pieces have descriptive, programmatic titles that invoke scenes from nature, fairy tales, or poetry. MacDowell commented that his works were "not written with the idea of describing the thing itself, but rather the atmosphere surrounding it." This method is in keeping with the principles of Impressionism, a late 19th-century movement in art and music that stressed mood and ambience over detail.

Edward MacDowell

MacDowell's superb pianism and years of teaching experience are reflected in his music. The passagework in his pieces "fits the hand," enabling developing pianists to achieve great speed and velocity. The most important aspect of Edward MacDowell's piano music, however, is its ability to communicate emotion and express what words cannot.

Fame in Europe and America

In the late 1880s, interest in American music in the United States brought about hundreds of concerts featuring American composers. Many of MacDowell's piano and orchestral works were performed and favorably reviewed in these concerts. In addition, MacDowell's pieces were published in the United States for the first time, and articles about the composer began appearing in music magazines and encyclopedias.

After 12 years in Europe, MacDowell moved to Boston in 1888 and began to teach piano and composition privately. Warmly received by the musical community, he performed his Second Piano Concerto with the Boston and New York Symphony Orchestras. Favorable reviews of the work and his playing led to his performing the concerto at the Paris Exposition of 1889.

MacDowell performed with immense dynamic range, from almost inaudible *pianissimos* to brilliant, sometimes harsh and percussive *fortissimos*. He was known for his exceptional speed and velocity, which enabled him to create Impressionistic "washes" of sound. During his years in Boston, he composed primarily for the piano, influenced by his teaching and by the demand for accessible music for amateur pianists.

MacDowell lived in cities all of his life, but he drew inspiration from time spent in the country. Due to the demands of his teaching and concert schedule, he did most of his composing during the summer months. In 1896, the MacDowells purchased an 80-acre farm in Peterborough, New Hampshire. MacDowell had a log cabin built in the woods near his new home, and it was here that he composed *Woodland Sketches*, one of his most famous works.

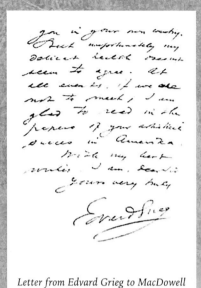

Letter from Edvard Grieg to MacDowell

About the Music

Sung Outside the Prince's Door (from *Forgotten Fairy Tales*), Op. 4, No. 1

- MacDowell enjoyed fairy tales and folklore, but this work is not related to a particular story.

- The song-like melody and the opening words *softly, wistfully* are key to interpreting this work.

- The B section of this ABA form is to be played "pleadingly." In measure 18, "reach" for the high note in the left-hand melody with a slight delay.

The Brook (from *Four Little Poems*), Op. 32, No. 2

- The poem that inspired this piece, "The Brook" by Robert Bulwer-Lytton (1831–1891), describes daydreaming by a brook while dropping pebbles in the water.

- The opening measures create a watery atmosphere by blending tones. The *mormorando* (murmuring) section that begins at measure 9 is marked by a thicker texture in the lower register.

- MacDowell believed that a poem could help the performer to interpret a work. Using imagination, perhaps the left hand in measures 17–18 illustrates pebbles being dropped in water, setting expanding rings in motion.

Scotch Poem (from *Six Poems after Heinrich Heine*), Op. 31, No. 2

- MacDowell's Scottish ancestry is on display in the poem he wrote that accompanies this tone painting.

- The music portrays a tempestuous sea and a harpist singing a sad song from the window of a castle.

- This piece makes frequent use of the "Scotch snap," a short accented note preceding a longer note (♪♩.).

To an Old White Pine (from *New England Idyls*), Op. 62, No. 7

- In the forest north of the MacDowell home in Peterborough, New Hampshire, stood a centuries-old pine tree that had been spared by early settlers when they cleared the land.

- The sight of this tree towering above its younger neighbors is depicted in the music by chords rising in a long crescendo.

- The quiet sections depict the sounds of the surrounding woods.

Improvisation (from *Twelve Virtuoso Studies*), Op. 46, No. 4

- This "improvisation" develops one theme (mm. 1–18) that is then repeated in a shortened version (mm. 19–32).

- Sweeping lines build intensity and urgency before peaking (mm. 13 and 30) and gradually releasing (mm. 14–18, 31–41).

- The pacing of dynamics and emotion between the lowest musical points (mm. 4 and 23) and highest musical points (mm. 13 and 30) of the long phrases is essential to the interpretation of this work.

Shadow Dance (from *Twelve Études*), Op. 39, No. 8

- Marian MacDowell described this piece as a work of "lightness and speed" reminiscent of a forest nymph that vanishes "before you know it."

- One of MacDowell's most popular works, this piece features a wide dynamic range (from *ppp* to *ff*) and aids in the development of finger dexterity and speed.

- Careful voicing is required to clarify lines in measures 7–8 and 57–58. Use of the sostenuto pedal in measures 28–44 helps clarify the thicker texture.

To a Water Lily (from *Woodland Sketches*), Op. 51, No. 6

- A horse and buggy ride in the country, during which the MacDowells came upon a pool covered with water lilies, inspired this piece.

- MacDowell's dynamics indicate different levels of sound with the notes on the lower staff played more quietly to blend with the sonority of the top two staves.

- The music is notated on three staves to make the wide spacing easier to read.

Hungarian (from *Twelve Études*), Op. 39, No. 12

- This piece makes use of rhythms and colors inspired by the *Hungarian Dances* of Johannes Brahms (1833–1897) and the *Hungarian Rhapsodies* of Franz Liszt (1811–1886).

- Technical challenges include fast scales, large leaps, martellato (hammered) chords, and frequent use of octaves.

- Marian MacDowell described this as "a virtuoso piece, to be played with dash and speed."

Excerpt from the manuscript of MacDowell's "Sonata Tragica"

Sung Outside the Prince's Door

from *Forgotten Fairy Tales*

Edward MacDowell (1860–1908)
Op. 4, No. 1

ⓐ If necessary, break this chord, playing the lower note ahead of the beat. Catch the lower note with the damper pedal.

The Brook
from *Four Little Poems*

Edward MacDowell (1860–1908)
Op. 32, No. 2

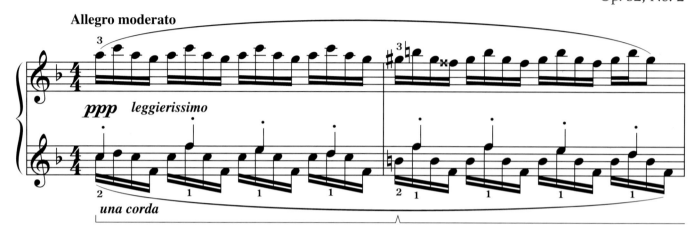

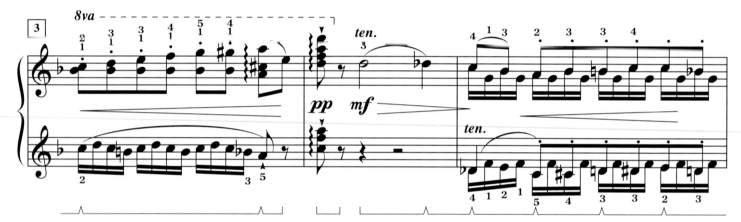

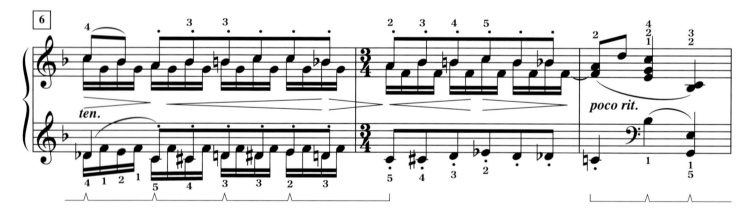

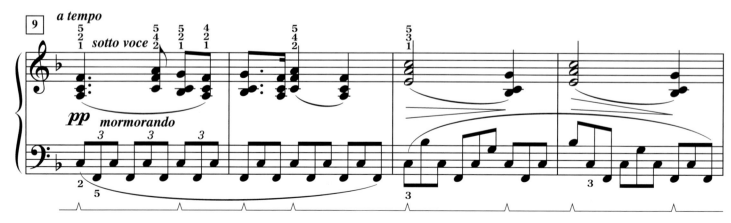

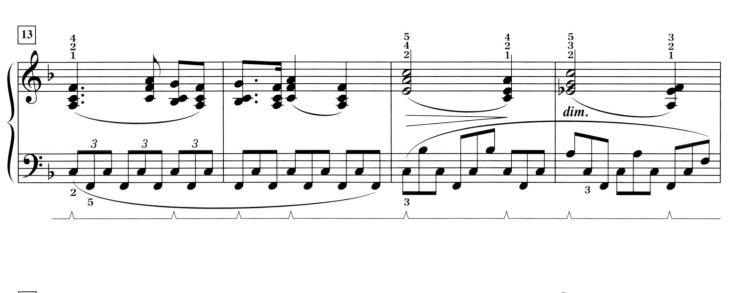

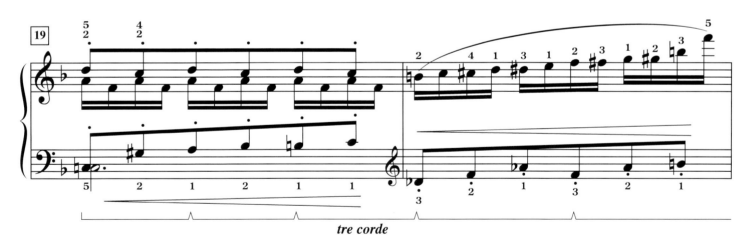

tre corde

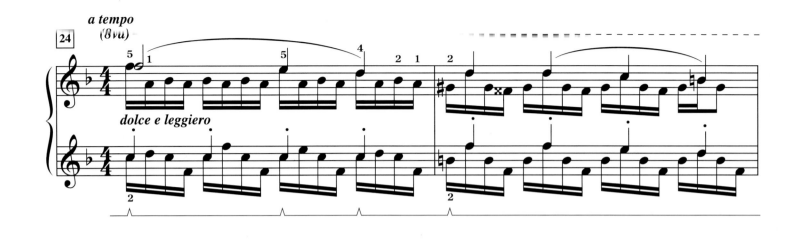

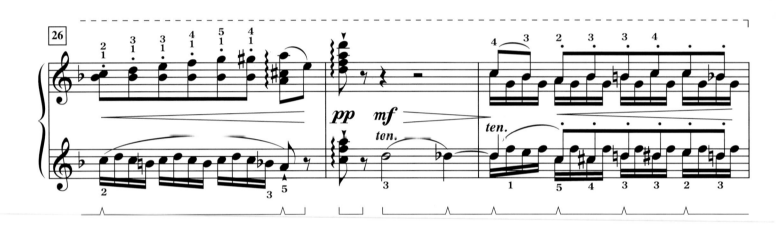

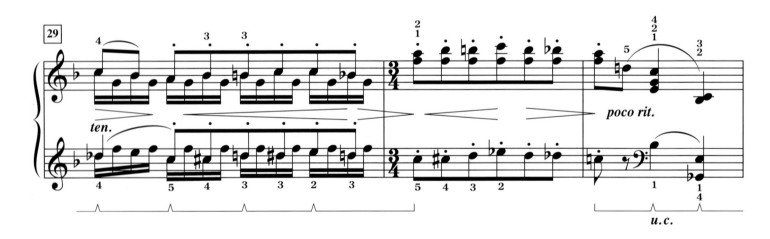

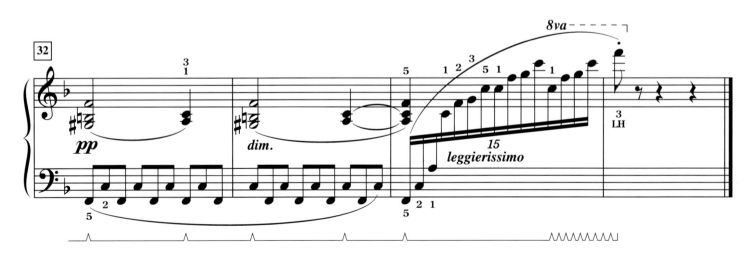

Scotch Poem

from *Six Poems after Heinrich Heine*

Far on Scotland's craggy shore
An old grey castle stands,
Braving the fierce North Sea;
And from the rugged casement
There peers a lovely face,

A woman's, white with woe.
She sweeps the harp strings sadly,
And sings a mournful strain;
The wind plays through her tresses,
And carries the song amain.

Edward MacDowell (1860–1908)
Op. 31, No. 2

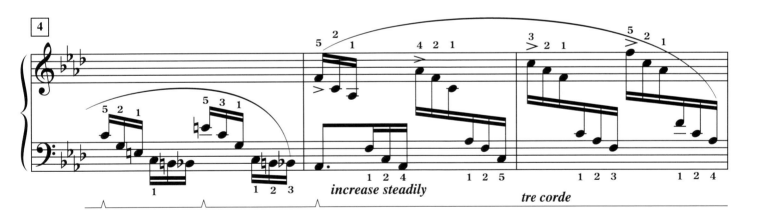

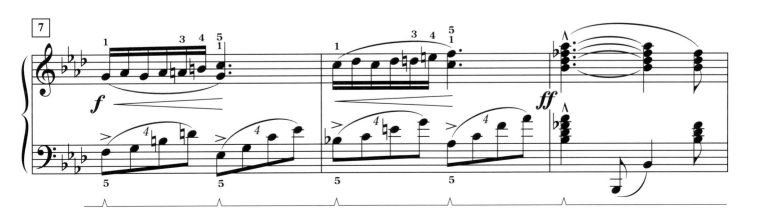

tre corde

8va - - - - - - - -

increase

ff

f

fff firmly

To an Old White Pine

from *New England Idyls*

A giant of an ancient race he stands, a stubborn sentinel
O'er swaying, gentle forest trees that whisper at his feet.

Edward MacDowell (1860–1908)
Op. 62, No. 7

Improvisation
from *Twelve Virtuoso Studies*

Edward MacDowell (1860–1908)
Op. 46, No. 4

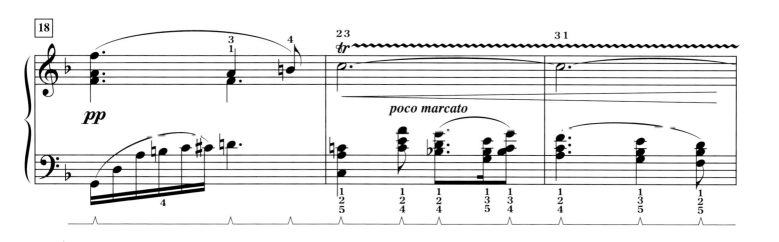

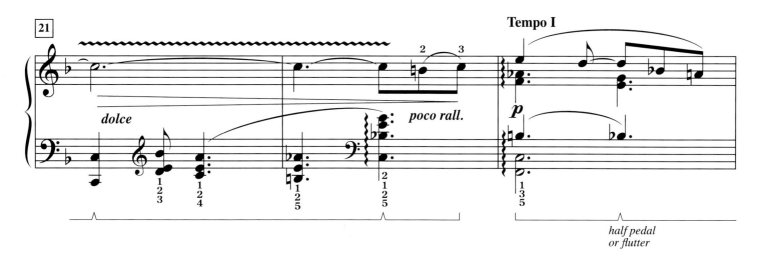

Shadow Dance

from *Twelve Études (for the Development of Technic and Style)*

(Speed, Lightness of Touch)

Edward MacDowell (1860–1908)
Op. 39, No. 8

This etude is to be studied *ppp* — with the wrist high and without lifting the fingers high.

Absolute equality both in tone and time is necessary. (MacDowell's instruction.)

To a Water Lily
from *Woodland Sketches*

Edward MacDowell (1860–1908)
Op. 51, No. 6

In dreamy, swaying rhythm ($\bd = 50$)

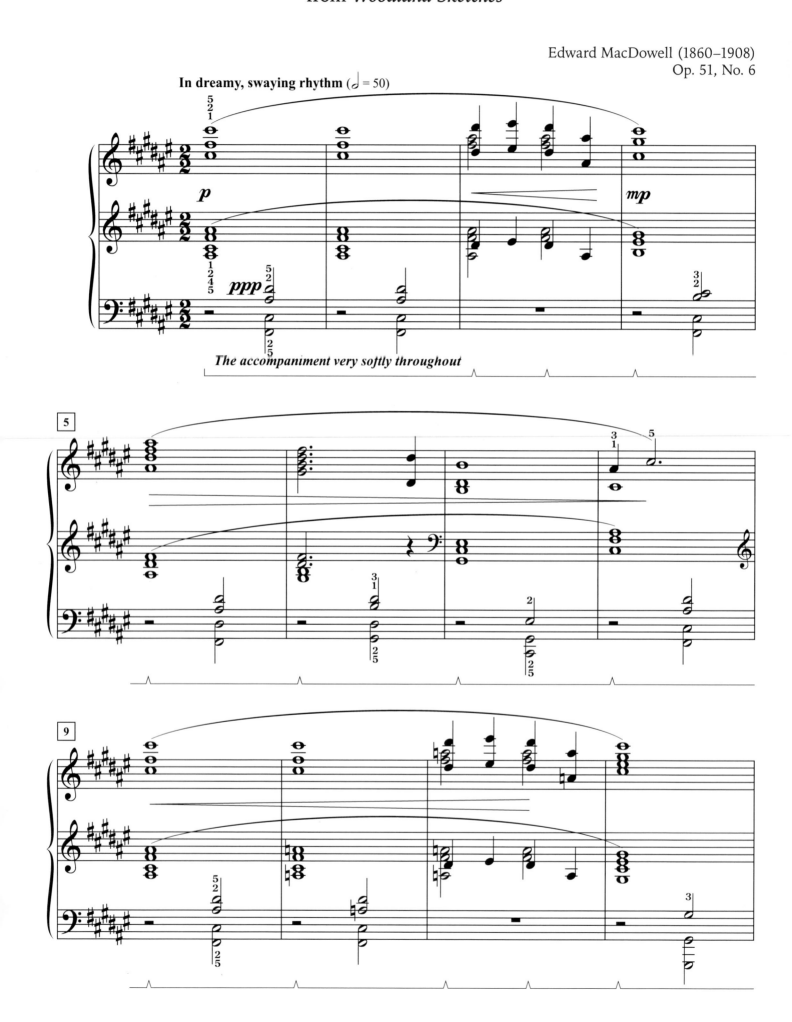

The accompaniment very softly throughout

27

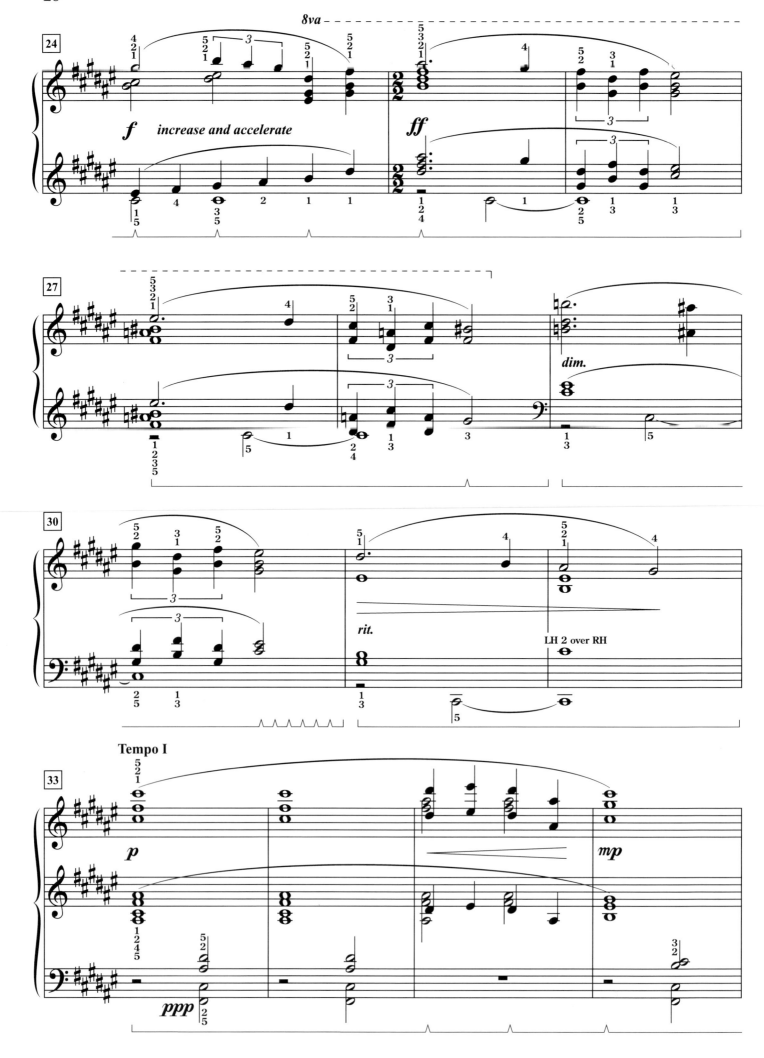

Hungarian

from *Twelve Études (for the Development of Technic and Style)*

(Dash, Speed, Virtuoso Playing)

Edward MacDowell (1860–1908)
Op. 39, No. 12